7 Steps to Flawless Communication
Copyright © 2015
Kass Thomas
ISBN: 978-0-9969039-0-5
All rights reserved.

Published by Kass Thomas - WWW.KASSTHOMAS.COM
Printed in the United States of America

FOREWORD

I was born and raised in the United States, in the historic town of Roxbury, Massachusetts. Located about ten minutes from downtown Boston, Roxbury is a melting pot of rich colors, languages and flavors from around the world.

I lived there until I was 18, when I left to attend college in New York City, an even bigger melting pot. With the exception of one year in Paris and lots of travel in between, New York City was my home for 15 years. I then moved to Rome, for love.

Over the years I've met all kinds of people, from all walks of life, race, color, creed, religion and political persuasion. No matter where a person comes from, what language they speak or what their particular situation is, there is one thing that continues to be abundantly clear to me:

There is so much more that unites us than separates us. When we are truly being ourselves, the ability to communicate with ease and establish true connection with everyone and everything on the planet, comes naturally to us.

This book literally woke me up one night and said "Write me, please. It's time to share with others what you know about communication. Show how easy flawless communication can be once you get in touch with the truth of you".

So here it is, my little book on flawless communication. It's short, it's simple and it's step by step. There's even a dedicated space to experiment with the steps and suggestions on how to use each one in *your* life. Use the 'milestones' section at the end of each step to record your successes. Write them down, then share them. Show others how easy it is to connect.

True connection starts with you, my dear. Have fun unveiling the flawless communication guru you truly are.

With love
Kass

This book was scheduled to go to print the week of retaliation bombings in Paris, France.

These acts of violence and those that proceeded them are a wake up call for all of us.

War is not the answer, violence is not the answer. We are the answer and here is the question:

What small act of kindness can each of us do every single day that will promote a culture of peace?

Be kind to you, your body and the things and people around you. Your small acts of kindness every day will have a ripple effect. You can and will contribute to a vibration of peace and create a different possibility here on planet earth.

Thank you in advance.

Kass Thomas
Paris, France
November 2015

*There is so much more that unites us
than separates us*

Index

PHASE I

CONNECTING

on connecting...

Often I meet people seeking information on how to relate to others with more ease, how to be better partners, employers or simply how to find more happiness. Yet, they themselves are strangely absent from their own lives.

They are missing in action, MIA, completely disconnected.

Sure anyone can get temporarily distracted or be momentarily in a fog while day dreaming, or something. But most people spend 900% of their time (that's right 900!), somewhere else other than the present moment and they are certainly not connected to themselves or their bodies.

Therefore, the first thing I recommend to everyone, before trying to connect with someone else, is to double check that you are connected to *you*.

These first two steps will help you connect to you!

Step 1

Show me the Magic!

Step 1: Show me the Magic!

I had been chasing behind this *being present* thing for years, trying to figure it out, get a grip on it, experience it, define it, ascertain whether I was really doing it or not.

Finally, one summer, I decided to take the situation into my own hands. I took a month off, got a small room near the beach, a beat up bicycle and decided I was going to learn how to simply BE PRESENT.

Every morning at dawn, I would ride my rickety, decrepit bike down the streets of Oak Bluffs to the beach at the Ink Well where I would meet The Polar Bears, a group of seniors who swam there every morning. I would swim with them at dawn in the ocean, communing with the fish at sunrise. It was beautiful.

When the Polar Bears left, I would get down to the business of BEING PRESENT. These "being present exercises" started with reading different books to find the right mantra for that day of the week, the right way to arrange the crystals for that phase of the moon and the best direction to face in order to meditate effectively at that latitude.

I did this routine for weeks and when I finally got back home to New York, and looked over my trip, I realized that the moments I was truly being present with me and being in communion with all things was when I was riding to the ocean each morning, singing with the birds, swimming with the fish and laughing with the Polar Bears.

I spent the whole summer looking for me and I was right there all along. All that time looking for the magic and all along it was right there with me!

What is it that you do, that gets you in touch with YOU?

HOMEWORK for
Step 1
Find the Magic

Once per day, for the next week: While performing a routine activity, take a few moments to ask yourself:

What magic can I find in this moment?

It may be while you are washing dishes, brushing your teeth, getting dressed or mowing the lawn.

Ask:
"Am I being me right now?"

"Is there any doing required?" (Is there anything required of me in this moment?)

MILESTONES for
Step 1
Show me the Magic

I found magic in the following "everyday" situations...

EXAMPLE:
a. while hanging out wet clothes I noticed the sun created a rainbow in a puddle
b. today I walked in rhythm with the raindrops, like a dance

Today I found Magic while...

Day 1: Today while....

Day 2:

Day 3:

Day 4:

Day 5:

Day 6:

Day 7:

Step 2

Talk to your body

Step 2: Talk to your body

Your body is talking, are you listening?
Your body has many different ways of communicating with you. What language does your body speak?

Your body is your friend and if you are willing to *listen*, it will give you a lot of information and help you with your flawless communication.

You can spend hours contemplating the right thing to say, what to do next *or* you can *simply* ask your body and get the answer *quickly* and *easily.* Sound good? Yea, I know.

Once you get the hang of listening to your body you will create more possibilities, increase your money flows, have more fun being around other people and even avoid unnecessary illness. Win-win.

I started this dialogue with my body years ago. Here's how: I would ask 3 questions that had either "yes" or "no" answers. They were either true or false. An example would be holding a cup in my hand and saying: this is a spoon, this is a knife, this is a cup and listening each time.

I would *listen* energetically to notice if there was any movement, any change, anything at all to indicate a difference between what was true and what was false.
What I noticed was that the truth made me feel lighter, and what was false made me feel heavier.

Try it out. It can change your life forever and make it way too easy!

The sensation of light or heavy is different for

everyone.

Sometimes you might not get a clear "yes" or "no", especially when you are asking questions that involve someone else or big decisions that are important to you.

That usually means that you are missing some information, or that you need to ask a different question.

HOMEWORK for
Step 2
Listen to your Body

Take 5 minutes each day this week to play: *Is it light or is it heavy?*

How does it work?
Make 3 statements. One true, the other two false. Then *listen! Where do you feel the truth in your body?*
Step 1. Relax;
Step 2. Hold a pencil in your hand;
Step 3. Say: "I have a pencil in my hand";
Step 4. *Listen* (see if you feel a "yes", meaning any lightness or expansion);
Step 5. Then say: "I have a cup of tea in my hand";
Step 6. *Listen* (any "no"? Does it feel heavy?);
Step 7. Then say "I have a lamp in my hand";
Step 8. "Listen".

MILESTONES Step 2
Talk to your Body

Practice this! Keep track of what shows up for you when you speak the truth and when you speak a non truth. Where do you feel it in your body?

With the truth I feel...
Example: lightheaded, opening in my chest....

With a lie I feel...

PHASE II

DIS-CONNECTING

about disconnecting...

It is important to have an easy and fast way of *disconnecting* from defensive posture, which keeps us separate from every *thing* and every *one*, including ourselves!

The lies, inventions and false positives that the mind feeds us on a daily basis distract us, making it difficult to remember who we really are and what is real and true for us.

We encounter new people or a new situation and we tend to keep them at arms length. We build up walls, hide behind masks and cover our true selves with a veil, in order to maintain a safe distance.

This distance ensures a lack of connection with others that eventually leads to boredom, a sense of profound sadness, despondency or depression.

These next two steps will help you quickly and easily *disconnect* from who you are *not*. They can alleviate stress, reduce anxiety and invite those tensions that you constantly carry around in your body to dissipate.

The exercises in the homework section will also help you quiet the mind.

In short, these steps are really cool.

Ready? O.K., here we go...

Step 3

Barriers Down

Step 3: Barriers Down

Pushing down the barriers exercise.

S tart with your hands above your head, palms facing down, and begin slowly pushing your palms toward the floor. Slowly.

S-L-O-W-E-R!!!!

Can you sense the tops of the barriers? If not that is ok, it still works. As you push your palms down slowly toward the floor, the barriers also come down, it's like magic.

If, however, you want to play with *sensing* what these barriers feel like and where they are exactly, simply notice at what height your hands start to resist or hesitate as they move slowly down toward the floor. It is subtle, but it's almost like you can *feel* where the barriers begin and end. Bounce your hands softly up and down a bit, as if you were playing with a sponge ball, but instead you are playing with the tops of these barriers.

With each centimeter or inch you gain, as your hands descend slowly toward the floor, if you *listen*, you can also perceive the tensions ease out of that *area* of your body that your hands are passing.

Let's try it again from the top. This time, as your hands come down past your forehead, feel the ruffled brow relax, sense the lines ease away toward your temples as they leave your forehead. If the tension does not go away automatically when your hands move past that part of your body, invite the tension to dissipate by repeating aloud or under your breath "barriers down, barriers down, barriers down". Remember this is an invitation *not* a command or an order. Sweet voice. Sweet talk. Sweet disconnect. You can even ask them please.

Sometimes I stop in mid air because I know that I have reached a place where the tension, the barriers, those walls are not moving. I take a deep breath, smile, sweet talk the barriers and invite them to go down just a tad bit more, beyond their comfort zone.

When I do this exercise, I usually try it again five minutes later. I notice the second time around that the barriers have gone down even more, all on their own.

Try it! Work with the barriers, negotiate. It is one of the most rewarding exercises you can do for your head, your heart, your body, oh yeah, and your life.

HOMEWORK for
Step 3
Push the Barriers Down

Once per day for the next week choose to push down your barriers.
It can be in a situation with someone you know who pushes your buttons, or with a total stranger. Usually parents, kids, coworkers, and ex husbands/wives work well.

Bonus: Use it in public, wherever you would normally go into reaction or defense, (trafic, rude salespeople) Instead of reacting, push down your barriers. Try it!

Things to remember:
1. breath;
2. don't force, invite;
3. feel the tension ease from your body
4. Try it again, 5 minutes later, see what changes.

MILESTONES for
Step 3
Barriers Down

Today I lowered my barriers in the following situations

1.
2.
3.

When I lowered my barriers **I noticed** ...

Example: (a difference in my body, their body; for the first time they smiled at me, or I saw, heard, felt; I was finally able to have a conversation with them without...)

1.
2.
3.

Step 4

Go beyond the Veil

Step 4: Go beyond the Veil

There is this invisible veil that many of us use to maintain a distance from others. It is not *us* that people see, it is this veil that we hide behind as if separation were truly possible. It is not. In order to construct a reality in which we believe separation is possible, we have to do a lot of contraction in our bodies and in our minds. It is exhausting and certainly does not help in our pursuit of flawless communication. In fact, it leads to *flawed* communication, loneliness, *dis*-ease and often depression.

The only place veils succeed in creating separation is in our minds where they create a distance between who we really are and the masks we wear, the veils we hide behind.

This is how it works: These masked versions of us slowly become who we think we are.

Then one fine day we begin to suspect that something is missing and then we discover that this something missing is *us*. We dare a sneak peak, out of the corner of our eyes, to see if we can catch a glimpse of us, but we have no idea where to look beyond that, how to find us, because the only *us* we know is well hidden, behind the mask, beyond the veil.

Many cultures and classes maintain the veil to preserve a demeanor or posture: the good wife; the perfect husband; the reliable source. These labels often find us living lives that have nothing to do with who we really are or what is truly important to us.

When you are able to disconnect the veil, come out from behind the mask and find the real you, you have more choice. Only then can you reconnect with your true nature and have more connection with you and everything and everyone else.

Goodbye walking dead. No more waiting for your number to be called.

You start actively living your life and making choices that create more for you and everyone around you. Being alive in your own life feels amazing. You feel amazing and you invite others to be alive in their lives too.

Yippee! Let the fun begin!

HOMEWORK for
step 4
Stepping Beyond the Veil

Twice per day, take a moment and simply count to 10. Do this when you first wake up and right before you go to sleep. Here's how it works:

1. Close your eyes
2. Put one hand on your heart and the other one on your stomach or solar plexus (whichever hand goes there naturally)
3. Sit down and feel your feet on the floor (if you must stand, that's ok too)
4. Count to ten, one number after the other
5. Don't forget to breath

We are good at being busy, doing, thinking, calculating. Stop a moment *and feel our own vibration.* What does your heart beat feel like?

n.b. No time frame on this one. You choose.

MILESTONES for
Step 4
Go Beyond the Veil

Today after counting to ten I was able to ...
example: hear different notes in the music, feel the breeze on my cheek, smell the coffee before it brewed...
1.
2.
3.

Today I went beyond the veil when I...
1.
2.
3.

I felt...
example: vulnerable, empowered, silly...
1.
2.
3.

PHASE III

RECONNECTING

Once we know who we are, connect to what is true for us and disconnect from what is not true for us, we start having more fun and enjoying everyone and everything around us in a whole new way. Our willingness to seek a different reality, beyond the controlled environment of the mind, is contagious and grows daily. **Reconnecting** with our natural capacity to commune with the animals, plants, fairies and people who inhabit this beautiful planet becomes easy.

In the next two steps you will engage your ability to communicate with the molecules and you will also learn how to quickly expand your zone. As you expand your zone and access more space, you experience a whole different level of communication.

You can also use these steps to better connect with your invisible and furry friends. Have fun being and receiving contribution everywhere and in all ways.

Step 5

Engage the Universe

Step 5: Engage the Universe

Normally when you are having trouble communicating with someone it is because they are blocking the flow of energy in some way or simply not being present.

Here's how you can get that energy flowing and invite them to be present with you. This tool of Access Consciousness® is really fun and it works like a charm in every area of your life: work, sex, relationship, business, etc.

Here's how it works.

When you encounter the **Energy Suckers - those people who** are always sucking energy from you, instead of resisting or succumbing and allowing them to exhaust you or suck the life out of you, simply flow energy towards them. That's right, don't resist, follow the energy. Contribute to their efforts. Go with the flow. Let them suck!

Does that mean that you allow them to suck like leaches until you are all dried up? No way! What I'm suggesting is that you not only stop resisting, but that you also help them out by flowing energy toward them. Say what?!?!? That's right.

How does it work?

When you are flowing energy to them, you're not just flowing energy from *you* and *your* body, oh no. You are pulling that energy from *behind* you, allowing the universe to contribute to you and give you strength. Now take that yummy energy that's flowing from the universe through you and allow it to flow toward *them*, then *through* them and finally back to the universe. The universe has got your back and theirs too!

With no more resistance on your part, they

can relax the intensity of their sucking. When they do, you will feel it in your body, no longer feeling exhausted. Once they relax their sucking, start pulling energy in the other direction, from behind *them*, through *them* and toward you. After a while you can open up the flow in both directions at the same time. This creates a simultaneity of flowing and pulling energy.

They feel better and become more present You feel better and the universe gets to play too. This allows the communication between you to go smoother. Win-win.

When instead you encounter **someone with their barriers up**, you start by first *pulling* energy from behind *them*, (engage the universe!), *through* them, toward you and through you. Again, they will relax and when they do, you can pull energy from behind *you*, through you, toward and through them.

This is easy. Simply pull as *hard* as you can, like you do when you *really* want to get someone's attention or when you are *willing* someone to look at you. Pull with *all* your might, with every pore of your being. Pull and flow energy and observe how the universe helps you out.

HOMEWORK for
Step 5
Creating Energy Flows

Over the next week, engage the universe at least once per day to create an energy flow.

First identify where the energy feels stuck with a person or in a situation.
Then ask:
What would get the energy flowing here?

Then ask:
Do I need to flow energy? And listen to your body. Is it light? Then engage the universe to pull energy from behind you (flow).

Is it heavy? Then engage the universe to pull energy from behind them (pull).

MILESTONES for
Step 5
Engage the Universe

Today I engaged the universe and played with creating energy flows when
Example: my boss was yelling at me and I pulled energy from behind her toward me, lowered my barriers and allowed it to go through me. Other examples...
1.
2.
3.

How was it different?
It was different because usually I would......
1.
2.
3.

Step 6

Expand your Zone
or
Connecting with your
INVISIBLE and FURRY FRIENDS

Step 6: Expand your Zone or Connecting with your INVISIBLE and FURRY FRIENDS

Observing and engaging with animals is perhaps the easiest way to grasp the magic and simplicity of flawless communication.

We two legged creatures tend to complicate communication, deny our feelings, ignore signs, postpone our needs and then use words to confuse and limit what is possible.

Animals, on the other hand, are quite clear: safety first, then, when there is no immediate danger, they either hunt, play, eat, or copulate … and then they rest.
Easy.

Instead of using our brains to create more choices, we have constructed a society with lots of rules and regulations to camouflage the basics. So we don't even know when it's time to hunt, eat, run or hide. This invokes all kinds of confusion and creates anxiety, stress and fear, making it difficult and often impossible to relate with anyone, even on a very basic level.

Be aware of this and expand your zone, go beyond the matrix, the constructed reality, and alleviate daily pressures that keep you separate and caught up in fear.

How does it work?:
Bring your attention to any area in your body where you feel some uncomfortable sensation. This sensation may show up as contraction, pain or simply a feeling. Begin breathing space into the center of that sensation. That's right. As if you were introducing a balloon and slowly blowing it up. Keep breathing space into the balloon and slowly expand the center of that area.

Expand it beyond your body, beyond the room you are in, beyond the building and beyond the town. Keep going until you feel a sense of space and that original sensation dissipates.

This is an easy and fast way to create more space around you and have a greater sense of peace in your mind, heart, environment and life. You can use it anywhere, anytime. You can also take your time with it, allowing your body to really languish in the sense of space this step invites.

Our bodies are full of space. Use this step to expand your zone and invite the space in your body to connect with the space that is all around you.

HOMEWORK for
Step 6
Expand the walls of your zone

Once per day, for the next week, take a moment to expand the walls of your zone.
Here's how:
Bring your attention to your solar plexus area (below your chest and above your stomach).

Put your hands out in front of you, palms facing one another, at the height of your solar plexus.

Imagine your hands are inside a tightly closed box.
Begin separating your hands slowly and as you do, imagine they are pushing out the sides of a tightly closed box which houses your solar plexus.

Keep expanding the space inside that box – on the left, right, above, below, in front of you and behind you. Expand the area of the box and as you do, expand the zone of your solar plexus, slowly separating your palms until your arms are fully extended and the box is a flat piece of cardboard. Then keep going, go beyond the walls of the room you are in, beyond the city limits and up to the sky and down into the earth and in every direction.

Remember to breath.

MILESTONES for
Step 6
Expand your Zone

You can ease the tension in your body, in that of an animal or in a room by using this "expand the zone" exercise.

Today I expanded the zone and brought ease to ...
Example: a cramp in my leg, an argument with my sister, a scared cat or a cranky bank teller...

1.
2.
3.
4.

PHASE IV

ESTABLISHING TRUE CONNECTION

Every molecule in the universe is in continuous communication with every other molecule in the universe.

When we are willing to see the **magic**, listen to our **bodies**, lower our **barriers**, **go beyond** the invented separation of the mind, **engage** the universe and **expand** our zone to **include** everyone and everything, then *establishing true connection* with each and every molecule in the universe is easy.

We are one of the great treasures of the universe, so is our beautiful planet and so is everything and everyone on it.

Once you've gone through the 7 steps, you begin to recognize that there is no "other" and that communion with every one and every thing already exists. It is from *that* space that all communication is flawless.

This final step will help you reconnect to the continuous joy of being alive and remind you that you can always establish *true connection* by connecting with the earth.

We have access to something beyond our physical form, something that supports us in everything we do and connects us to everything we are.

There is so much more that unites us than separates us.

Enjoy your life and celebrate your true connection with everything that is!

Step 7

Connect with the Earth

Step 7: Connect with the Earth

The earth is an amazing and incredibly magical place. It provides nurturing, nourishment, shelter, entertainment, heat, curiosity, mystery, miracles and more. The earth is an intricate source of endless wonder. What can we learn from her grace?

There is so much gentle potency available to us when we are willing to tap into the vast resources that the earth provides.

So many people have so many points of view about what the earth needs, what it doesn't need and what's the best way to take care of the planet.

I believe that if we take care of *ourselves* then the earth gets taken care of as well.

Recognizing the **Magic** in everyday

expressions of the earth is a gift. The sunrise, sunset, dawn... I mean really: have you ever seen something so simple yet so beautiful? You don't even have to see it, just talking about it, reading about it and knowing it's coming is already so exciting.

Asking for clarity on what is right and light for us and listening to our **Body** is a way of acknowledging the earth, the universe.

Lowering our Barriers allows us to gift to the earth and receive from the earth with more ease.

Going beyond the superficial, walking in nature, connecting with the trees, their vibration, gets us in touch with our own vibration and that of the earth.

Creating a flow where there is stagnation and **expanding** the energy when it is contracted regenerates and breathes life into both you and the earth.

Expand the zone of those animals, trees, plants and people who walk around on the earth tense and dense and scared. Expand them so that they too can receive and be the contribution.

Know that the **earth** needs you and you need the earth and that you are a vital part of any sustainable future here. Being willing to connect with the earth will invite grace, peace and joy into your life and the flowers will bloom just for you as their way to say thank you.

This is your flawless communication.

You are the drop of water and you are the ocean. Be the source in your own life and all will connect and gift to you, with ease.

HOMEWORK for
Step 7
Pull the Energy of the Earth through your Body

Put your feet on the ground, close your eyes and bring your attention to the center of the earth, the core.
Get the intensity of the earth's core and imagine two strings coming up from the center of the earth, breaking the earth's surface.

Pull those into the soles of your feet.
These two strings, connected to the center of the earth enter into your feet, **pass your ankles and travel up your legs,** uniting at your abdominal area as they continue traveling past your heart, up your neck and up and out of the top of your head.

Imagine this string that starts from the center of the earth and connects with every star and every space between every star in the universe, through you.

MILESTONES for
Step 7
Connect with the Earth

Each day, at least once, connect with the earth. Each time you connect, notice how much easier it gets, how quickly you succeed and the different ways in which the earth lets you know that you are connected.

Today I stopped to have a conversation with a....
examples: person who I usually never speak to, a tree, my plants, a cat...

Today I felt the presence of the earth as I communicated with...
examples: my body, my dog, my mom...

A NOTE FROM ME

What's next?

These 7 steps to flawless communication can be used one by one or all together.

Sometimes it is one step, sometimes it is a combination of steps and sometimes just thinking about the steps will already change the situation.

The key is to use them and recognize how easily they can transform what is going on for you in any given moment. You can use them to turn a situation into something that works better for you and creates more possibilities. Once you have played with each of these steps, you will become familiar with the vibration they create and you will instinctively know which step to call upon to create the change you are looking for.

Enjoy these steps and have fun exploring the ease of flawless communication with everyone and everything around you.

Kass

P.S.

If you enjoyed this book and would like to play more with these steps, or know more about my workshops in general, you can find me at WWW.KASSTHOMAS.COM *or at* KASSTHOMAS.ACCESSCONSCIOUSNESS.COM

I am available on line for private sessions, group training or just to say hello.

If you would like to know more about Access Consciousness® visit: ACCESSCONSCIOUSNESS.COM

I also travel around the world offering workshops and seminars so perhaps we will meet in person somewhere, someday.

There is so much more that connects us than separates us.

So look me up and let's connect.

It's easy!

Made in the USA
Lexington, KY
11 January 2017